The 2004 Indian Ocean Earthquake and Tsu:
Natural Disaster of the 2. _____

By Charles River Editors

Aerial photo of damage done in Indonesia

About Charles River Editors

Charles River Editors provides superior editing and original writing services across the digital publishing industry, with the expertise to create digital content for publishers across a vast range of subject matter. In addition to providing original digital content for third party publishers, we also republish civilization's greatest literary works, bringing them to new generations of readers via ebooks.

Sign up here to receive updates about free books as we publish them, and visit Our Kindle Author Page to browse today's free promotions and our most recently published Kindle titles.

Introduction

Photo of the tsunami hitting Thailand

The 2004 Indian Ocean Earthquake and Tsunami (December 26, 2004)

"Whenever an earthquake or tsunami takes thousands of innocent lives, a shocked world talks of little else." - Anne M. Mulcahy

In the Christian world, December 25 is a time of great rejoicing and celebrating the birth of Jesus Christ. It is by far the most festive time of year, marked by parties, church services and giving gifts. It is also a popular vacation time, as families use the breaks given by offices and schools to travel, often to exotic destinations. That is why so many of those who witnessed the Great Tsunami of 2004 were not native to the areas struck but had traveled there to enjoy the sun during the dead of winter. Most of them slept soundly on Christmas night and woke up the following morning with plans to enjoy a fun day playing along white beaches or exploring dense jungles. For many, it was supposed to be the adventure of a lifetime, but for everyone in the region, it would instead become a fight for survival.

Around 8:00 a.m. on December 26, a massive earthquake registering a 9.1-9.3 on the Richter Scale struck off of Sumatra, Indonesia, making it the 3rd strongest earthquake ever recorded by seismographs. On top of that, the earthquake shook for nearly 10 minutes and generated incredibly strong tsunami waves, some of which topped out at over 100 feet tall as they crashed inland in places like Thailand, India, and Indonesia. Given the great distances traveled, some of the tsunami waves didn't reach shore until 7 hours after the earthquake, but thanks to the element of surprise, people in the region had virtually no warning of what was coming. With more energy than that generated by every weapon and bomb used during World War II combined, the tsunami waves pulverized entire towns and swept away hundreds of thousands of people across Southeast Asia, in addition to displacing more than a million people.

Given how calamitous the events were, a massive outpouring of humanitarian support was sent to the affected areas, and over $10 billion was poured into relief efforts. Not surprisingly, a better tsunami detection system was also designed to prevent against any similar occurrence, even though it's believed that the last similar event in that region took place over 500 years earlier. *The 2004 Indian Ocean Earthquake and Tsunami: The Story of the Deadliest Natural Disaster of the 21st Century* chronicles the incredibly powerful earthquake and the deadly tsunami waves it triggered in Southeast Asia. Along with pictures of important people, places, and events, you will learn about the 2004 earthquake and tsunami like never before, in no time at all.

The 2004 Indian Ocean Earthquake and Tsunami: The Story of the Deadliest Natural Disaster of the 21st Century

About Charles River Editors

Introduction

Chapter 1: Just a Twinge

Chapter 2: The Ocean Pulled Back

Chapter 3: The Bay Began to Fill

Chapter 4: Wiping Out Everything It Touched

Chapter 5: The Life Taking Swell

Chapter 6: Bloodied and Battered People

Chapter 7: Taken to a Hospital

Chapter 8: Back to Reality

Bibliography

Chapter 1: Just a Twinge

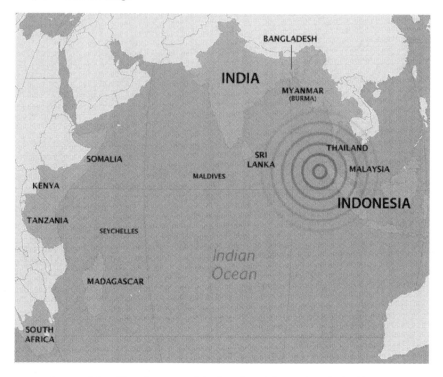

A map of the affected areas and the location of the earthquake's epicenter

"For the earth, it was just a twinge. Last Dec. 26, at 7:59 a.m., one part of the planet's undersea crust made an abrupt shift beneath another along a 750-mile seam near the island of Sumatra. The tectonic plates had been grating against each other for millenniums, and now the higher of the two was lifted perhaps 60 feet. For a planet where landmasses are in constant motion across geological time, the event was of no great moment. But for people - who mark the calendar in days and months rather than eons - a monumental catastrophe had begun, not only the largest earthquake in 40 years but also the displacement of billions of tons of water, unleashing a series of mammoth waves: a tsunami." - Barry Bearak, author of *The Day the Sea Came*

Those who monitor such things knew something bad had happened when, just before 8:00 in the morning on December 26, the alarms went off at earthquake monitoring stations in the area. People jumped to their equipment, looked once and then again to verify what they were seeing, and then grabbed their phones and called fellow scientists to verify the information they were getting. Equipment all over the world agreed that a massive earthquake, registering somewhere between 8.9-9.3, had taken place in the depths of the Indian Ocean. While there is still debate over its exact Richter Scale rating, it was the third strongest earthquake to ever be recorded, and tectonic activity extended across over 800 miles as the Indian Plate was subducted underneath the Burma Plate.

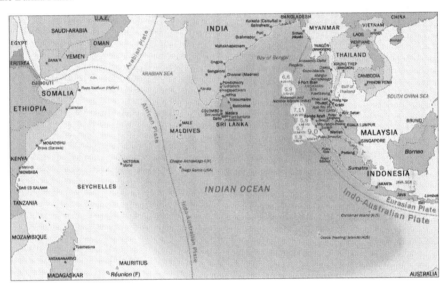

A map of major tectonic plates in the region

As seismologists compared data and made observations, people were going about their daily lives across Southeast Asia. Mark Brandon was touring Asia with two friends and was on the coast of Thailand that morning. He recalled, "I think it was around 8am when the earthquake struck. Having just come from Taiwan, where earthquakes occur regularly, this quake was rather a surprise, especially as there are no plate lines around Thailand. So wherever it came from, I knew it was a big one. The whole bungalow shook for a good 30 seconds and this was at ground floor level. I went back to sleep and got up around 9am. Coffee was on my mind, as it is most mornings, and I gave the earthquake no more thought. I got changed into my T-shirt, shorts and flip-flops; picked up my phone, wallet and sunglasses and headed to the resort's beach restaurant."

Indeed, not only was the earthquake powerful, it was also long. Shaking the depths of the earth for more than eight minutes, it lasted longer than any other quake ever recorded. Nonetheless, people who were so far away from the epicenter didn't understand the strength or duration of the quake, or the subsequent tsunami waves that would follow. Sally Huyton was also in Thailand

and had been up late on Christmas, enjoying more than the normal number of drinks she typically consumed. She was with her family and was looking forward to spending December 26, Boxing Day to those from the United Kingdom, swimming and soaking up some sun. She had no idea that her plans would soon be interrupted: "On Boxing Day morning, I think it was about 8ish, we were awoken by an earthquake. We weren't too sure what it was at first as we had had a few drinks the night before and thought we may still have been drunk. Paul got up and saw that the lamp in the corner was shaking all over the place. I don't know how long it lasted but as we were awake now we thought we would get up. We were always in bed when breakfast was being served so we thought we'd give it a try. ... The rest of us sat round talking about the earthquake, not realizing the other effects it has. When we had finished, I wanted to go to the chemist and get some cream for my jellyfish stings...."

The quake was felt all around the sunny coast of the Indian Ocean, and even as far away as cold Alaska. Ye Tun and her family felt the earthquake in Yangon, Myanmar. She later wrote, "My family was sleeping soundly and I felt my body was floating then I heard the sound of crushing glasses on the refrigerator, the water in the tank flew out and I knew that was an earthquake. I also heard the loud shouting of my neighbors. All the members of my family woke up and we all ran to the ground floor as our eight-story building was shaking. My poor grandmother could not run and she was afraid. We have never had any experience of earthquake. After a few minutes the ground stopped shaking."

The quake was also felt in India, where it damaged buildings even before the tsunami hit. Geeta Pandey and her family were on the Indian coast when it hit, and she wrote, "We had just boarded a ship in Port Blair, the capital of the Andamans and Nicobar Islands, when the earthquake struck. As it pulled out - I was standing on the lower deck - when I saw the jetty crumble just below me. We had absolutely no idea what happened. I had no idea that it was an earthquake until I was told by the ship's captain. Damage on the islands has been extensive. We have no power - we are told it will be days before it will be restored."

Most people assumed that the quake, at least as they felt it on land, was no big deal. While there was a distinct tremor, the coastline where people lived was so far from the epicenter that it felt more like a soft rattle than the kind of dangerous, life-changing quake that it actually was. Mark Oberle, who was staying on Patong Beach in Phuket, later admitted, "We slept in late, but about 8AM we were awoken by the bed shaking for 2-3 minutes. It was clear this was an earthquake, followed 20 minutes later by another. Because this is not a region of major quakes, I just assumed that they were small, local quakes. The possibility of a tsunami never crossed my mind."

Chapter 2: The Ocean Pulled Back

"At first - the ocean pulled back. It was as if somewhere way out at sea - a god pulled a giant plug on the bathtub. The water was sucked backwards - leaving only a muddy potholed ground -

full of flopping fish - and small holes of water. All of the seniors and families (mostly the ones on the beach at 9:00 in the morning), decided it was a great time to explore this unique moment. They walked out and looked at the new landscape. They explored trinkets never seen before as this part of the ocean bed had never been exposed in 50 years. Children bounced along to little pools of water - newly created children's pools just perfect for jumping in. The turned their backs to the distance. And yet others slept on the beach - taking in the cool and pleasant morning air." - Rick Von Feldt

Sunday morning, December 26, dawned brightly off the coast of Sumatra. As the sun rose, those who had come to the beach early to fish or run or just enjoy nature's morning show had no way of knowing that, within a few short hours, their lives would be changed forever. Nonetheless, even as people put on sunscreen and fishermen headed for open waters, their destinies were already sealed by a rising force that was already underway in the depths of the Indian Ocean. A woman named Fiona and her husband, Simon, were on the tiny island of Ko Hong just off the coast of Thailand, admiring the unique beauty of the landscape in the last moments before the disaster. She described the scene: "We got the Ko Hong…sometime after 10am I presume…. Ko Hong has a double bay. The first part of the bay (the part where we parked the boat) consists of a narrow beach leading to sheer cliffs. In between the two bays is a limestone karst about 30 feet tall, and when you walk around the karst you reach the second bay which is probably one of the most beautiful places I have ever seen in my life – your classic white beach, completely clear water, with trees lining it. Anyway, we all got out of our boat and started walking towards to second bay, which would apparently have led us to the lagoon and our canoes. … At this point we were just about up to the beach of the second bay, and everybody else was walking through the little forest towards the canoes. There were 120 people on the island that day."

Rick Von Feldt had arrived on Phuket, a small island off the coast of Thailand, at 9:00 on the morning of December 26, but as he drove along the coastline, he looked out over the water and noticed something strange. As he wrote, "I notice that there was - well - no water. Now that is certainly odd. I thought it odd. And I remembered thinking – 'was the tide pool that strong the last time I was there?' My driver seemed to be puzzled as well - and was saying something in Thai - but I didn't pay much attention."

Things still seemed strange when he reached his hotel, high on a hill overlooking the ocean: "As I went to sit in the open air bar - overlooking the bay - I noticed that all of the staff of the hotels were crowding on the edge -also looking over the bay. This caused the guests to wonder as well - and we all came to the edge - looking to see what they were seeing. I asked one of them, 'What are you seeing?' 'Water! The Water!' they said. Hmmm. They also noticed that all of the water had gone away. Or at least - most had receded out of the bay. Boats were suddenly grounded. And people dotted the beach in perplexity."

A picture of the receding water line in Phuket, Thailand before the tsunami waves

What Van Feldt and the others did not realize they were seeing was the first warning signs of a severe tsunami, for the earthquake had disturbed the ocean floor so violently that it had responded by sucking millions of gallons of water out from the coastline, all in preparation for throwing it back on the coast with a murderous vengeance. Luke Simmonds was also on vacation on Phuket, traveling with a group of friends, one of whom was named Lars. Simmonds remembered, "At about 10:30 we went to the beach. Lars and I planned to go sailing, but there was no wind so we opted for water skiing. We waited for the boat and noted the wind was picking up so we would sail afterwards. First Lars skied and then it was my turn. At the moment I got into the water the lagoon started to drain out - in particular on the far right hand side of the bay (as you look out to sea). Within seconds it was too shallow to ski, so I climbed back into the boat. Lars, I and the driver sat there just watching the water drain away without any comprehension of what was to happen next. At first we saw a couple on a Kayak struggling in the current - they were being sucked out to sea. But then almost immediately they were on the top of a small wave kayaking into the beach at some speed. We were excited by the site and just imagined they were having some fun. Of course we could not know of the huge volume of water that was underneath them that once it reached the shallow water would simply rise up into a huge wave. That is basically what happened next."

Indeed, the wave that Simmonds initially observed was no ordinary wave; it had traveled hundreds of miles from the very site of the earthquake itself. Boaters would later recall experiencing a seemingly small, harmless rise in the water, but what few if any realized was that the rise was actually just the surface of a giant liquid vortex rushing towards shores at hundreds of miles per hour.

Others around the world on coasts bordering the Indian Ocean were experiencing the same thing. In Colombo, Sri Lanka, Jayarine Saldin-Lyne observed, "We were in Beruwela - Hotel Confifi. Although we planned to leave at 8AM we were delayed by an hour or so, searching for the car keys. It was a beautiful day with the sun shining brilliantly. Suddenly we came upon the people of the area who looked all flustered and were running hither and thither carrying bags and babies. A motorist shouted to us that the roads were closed and that 'the sea had come in.' So we decided to turn back."

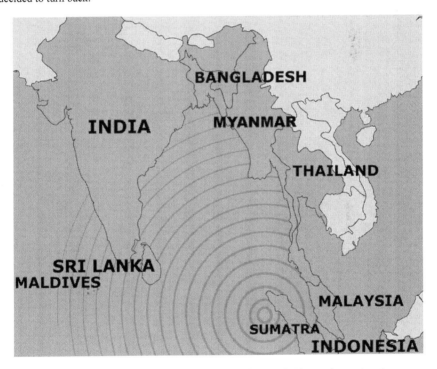

Back in Thailand, from his vantage point near the beach, Von Feldt saw the wave as it approached, but at the time he had no understanding of what he was seeing and could not comprehend its size, speed, or power. "At first - you saw it. The horizon began to be blocked out - and you saw a blue-black dark wall spring to life. You could tell the water was coming back. And soon, all of your newly discovered play areas would be back to normal - covered once again by water. Sure, it felt odd. And you wondered, 'Why is this happening.' But no logical reason came to mind. It was a full moon last night - and so perhaps the moon was creating an abnormal tide. Most of us didn't live by oceans - and so we had no clue as to how the ocean was really supposed to work. Many locals stood up at the retaining wall - in awe - looking at their backyard sea of water that was no more. But they knew the power of the ocean - and like a man who had once been bit by a snake, were fearful to get any closer. But there were fish. Flopping large fish. Laying there. Perfect for a fry or bake. How could you let them just lie there? And so, a few local came out to explore. And if the locals were out there - then surely they must know why this was happening. And so surely it must also be safe?"

Chapter 3: The Bay Began to Fill

"But then we saw the wall. … And then we could see it was moving too fast. For a few seconds, everyone was mesmerized by the wall. And the sound. And then, with a snap of a finger, hundreds were popped out of their hypnosis - and people started to walk. Fast. And then run. And soon, everyone started to scream. 'Get up on the wall!' some shouted. … And some thought it would be ok if you just got up on the wall. The water filled up the beach like a gorging bathtub. Water came at the people at 150 mph - and no matter how hard you tried, unless you were close to the wall - you couldn't outrun it. … Some people stumbled. Some held their ground or were swept with the water towards the wall. People sputtered and coughed. The water spilled over the road. Some people went down - and most were in shock to have seen such a thing happen. But that was only the beginning. And while many people were able to stand back up again - bruised and battered, or having had all of their clothing ripped off by such a fast and switch wave - it wasn't over." - Rick von Feldt

It is often difficult for people to predict the best place to endure a crisis, but in the case of tsunami waves as large as the ones generated by the earthquake, there was simply no good place to be. The stories told by survivors came from many places in many different countries. For instance, Luke Simmonds was still in the fishing boat when the wave hit: "We were in the ski boat facing towards the shore, when the water passing underneath us began to pull the boat around and towards the shore. Almost out of nowhere there was a huge wall of water, behind us at the beach. We were at the bottom of a 10 meter wave that stretched the entire length of the beach, maybe 1km. I said to Lars that we were in trouble - at this moment it didn't even dawn on me that the wave would pass through the island causing the destruction that it did. I screamed at the driver to get us out to sea, but even at full power, the boat just got sucked to the bottom of the wave. The wave collapsed on the top of the boat. I remember covering my head and rolling into a ball. Underwater I just kept on thinking 'please don't get hit by something.' I came to the surface, breathed, and then was pulled under again."

What Simmonds did not realize (and what many don't understand) is that what is perceived as a wave is really the crest of a circular moving wall of water that rolls over and over again like a wheel. As a result, Simmonds was caught like a leaf in the spoke of a bicycle tire, destined to go around and around until he broke free, but fortunately, he had experience on his side. He explained, "I like to think that all of the diving I have done helped me - I knew not to fight the current and to wait as long as I could before reacting. The truth is, I was just lucky. I came to the surface, grabbed some more air, and then saw a huge wave coming at me. I could see that it wasn't about to break where I was so I took a breath and dived through it, coming up the other side. I grabbed some wood to hang onto, but then saw a life jacket (presumably from our boat) floating 10 meters away. I swam like crazy for it - in my head I knew it was the best thing to do. I got it on and instantly felt safe - I was afloat in the sea and things didn't look that bad for me. I knew I was safe from drowning I just had to wait for help. I looked for Lars, saw our driver first, and then Lars about 150 meters away, he looked unhurt, but even from that distance I could see his face had taken on a different aspect. I have thought about this since and have decided that it was survival."

Picture of water coming ashore in Phuket, Thailand

Though Thailand was among the worst hit by the wave, more than 10 separate nations around the Indian Ocean were affected by the tsunami. Thousands of miles away in Colombo, Sri Lanka, a woman named Ruwanthi Senarathne was shocked to find herself in the middle of a life-threatening crisis. She later wrote, "My husband, my child and myself were driving along the coast in our car. Then we saw lot of people gathered at the beach and some were running along the coastal line too. We asked what happened, they told us the sea came on to the road. At the time we just thought it may be a common thing, but then suddenly two men came running in front of the vehicle and told us to turn. People had very confused emotions and nobody knew what to do next. We saw the wave strike just 100 meters away from us."

By this time, on Ko Hong, Fiona and Simon were also becoming aware that something was wrong, though they did not initially realize how serious the situation was. Fiona explained, "I remember looking out into the sea and seeing a line of water coming towards us, obviously a big wave. Then all the Thai people started running. At this point I didn't feel any urgency at all – it was almost like a dream. Somebody – I think it must have been Si, shouted at me 'RUN' and so I started running. There was still absolutely no urgency at all about me, and I remember checking my handbag to make sure that it was firmly attached to me in case anything (I didn't know what) happened. After about 5 paces my right flip flop fell off, and I stopped to put it back on."

As Fiona was hesitating over her next move, across the Indian Ocean in Bangladesh, people had no time to think, especially if they were caught near the ocean's edge. One resident from Chittagong recalled, "Me and my sister were near the port when we felt a sudden movement beneath our feet. We then saw people screaming and running away from the coast. There were huge tidal waves about two meters high crashing against the port. We were really scared. It was as if the sea was swallowing the land from every direction." Sultana Azam also experienced the tsunami's arrival from a very precarious position: "I was at the beach during the time this tragedy occurred. I was playing on the beach with my sister when we felt along with others on the beach the ground moving beneath our feet. We then saw [a] huge tidal wave about 1.5m heading straight towards the coast. Everyone panicked and fled as soon as possible."

Naomi Bowman was lying on the beach that morning when she was startled by an ominous sight. "26th December was another beautiful sunny day and at about 10:20 am I was on Charlie beach on Koh Phi Phi island, reading a book with my headphones on when I looked round to see a few people running and shouting. Looking out to sea I saw in the distance about an inch high of dark brown water travelling towards the beach. I thought that the tide was coming in, although it wasn't slowing down and was obviously the wrong color. By the time I stood up with my bag the water was already past my feet. I started running but it was knee height now and so fast it knocked over a woman running ahead of me. Holding onto a palm tree to stop myself falling, I looked out into the waves, now thinking it must be some kind of tropical storm. I was really frightened, dropped everything and ran again. A few seconds later waves smashed into my back and took me under the water. For the first time the word tsunami came into my head."

It is often difficult for someone who has been through a traumatic event to cope with the idea of how quickly life, and priorities, can change. Sally Huyton wanted to pick up a few items before she walked down to the beach, a trip she would never make: "On our way to the chemist we decided to go via the pool to see Matt. When we got there he was on a sunbed with his headphones on listening to music with his back to the sea. Our pool was right on the beach, about 3ft up. Paul started talking to Matt as I stood looking out at the bay. Then I noticed this big wall of what looked like white water but was a dirty dark gray color stretching from one side of the bay to the other. I shouted to the boys to come and have a look … We all stood at the side of the pool watching it in amazement. Paul said 'It's a tsunami,' but it didn't look threatening at all, it was just weird. There was a wooden longboat and a speedboat which started to get pushed by this water towards each other, it was only then that we thought 'Oh my god, the people on those boats could die if they collide.' Whilst we were watching that, we didn't realize that the water in front of us was rapidly rising. The wall of water that was coming in was pushing the water that was in the bay up."

One of the most frightening things about the tsunami for many people was that it happened when they were far from home in a country where they did not know the geography or understand the language. Pate Benton and her family experienced it in Khao Lak, Thailand: "We walked along the road about 50 yards when suddenly people started running around excitedly, then cars started hooting and motor bikes rushing about, then screaming started. We obviously knew something was wrong and tried to convey the question. Someone shouted landslide, landslide, so we thought there'd been an accident up the road or something. But everyone was in such a panic we rushed back to the dive master hut and David was outside. We woke Anthony and his girlfriend, Lei, and we all walked up the road a bit. Suddenly, injured people started coming up from the beach – the first person we saw was a man with all the skin gone from his front. Then obviously the word got about that there'd been a giant wave."

Chapter 4: Wiping Out Everything It Touched

"We walked from our beach on one side of Phi Phi, down the narrow lane lined with shops and shacks, to the pier on the other side. We stood for a minute, waiting to get on the longboat we'd just hired to take us to Monkey Island. While we were waiting we noticed that the bamboo jetty on our left was collapsing into the sea. People were jumping off it and the longboat men were jumping into their boats, which immediately flipped over. People were pointing at the sea and Zac (my 10yr old son) asked if there was a shark. There was a sudden sense of panic in the air and I said, 'Let's go' and we started to walk back up the lane, away from the pier. Within seconds there was a lot of shouting and everyone started running. I still didn't know what was happening but I knew it was serious. I heard a huge roar and when I looked back there was a massive wave rushing down the lane behind us, wiping out everything it touched. We turned right into another lane and were immediately stuck in a people-jam (we later realized that this lane lead to the Phi Phi Hotel, one of the only tall, concrete buildings on the island)." - Felix in

Phi Phi

While those on the beach and in the streets were the first to see the tsunami wave, many people were in their offices working, when it hit. Dave Lowe was one of them, and he later wrote, "It was just after 11.00 am, a perfect Maldives day, 90 degrees, sunny, and no clouds. I was in my office working, at the northern end of the island, which was 20 meters across, fighting a hangover from a hard night in the bar that had stretched to 4 am. I was woken up that morning at 7 am by an earthquake, but being from California, it seemed like nothing, and I did not even think of a tsunami. I was half listening to a colleague whine about a missing pen, then I heard a strange bump against the door, and people outside were screaming, 'The children! The children!' ... I leapt to the door to find seawater seeping under it, and it took all my strength to push it open. when I looked outside, I could see that the ocean was now level with our island, and to my horror, a wall of water, boiling, frothing, angry as hell, was bearing straight down at us...there was a strange smell in the air, like death, and a weird mist that looked like thick fog...I stopped breathing, and ran."

One thing that always strikes people in the midst of a crisis is the strange number of things that do and do not get destroyed. A man named Patrick was also working in Maldives that day on the South Ari atoll, a mecca for wealthy tourists planning to enjoy a long relaxing day of sun and pampering. He noted, "I was working at a resort in the Maldives. At 11:00 the sea started to rise and suddenly guests and staff were fighting for our lives: the waves got so high some were nearly washed out to sea. All of our rooms were destroyed. To our horror the wave came back again, from the opposite direction, and smashed us again."

Rahul Thiagarajan was vacationing with his family in Chennai, a resort area of his native India, when they encountered the life-threatening wave. Later, he remembered how they only barely survived: "My wife and my eldest daughter were in our hotel room on the first floor in Mahabalipuram when a monster wave came in the window. I could hear them screaming and two village men came running to help but the floor split into two, leaving cracks in between and my wife's leg got stuck inside. My wife was pulling my daughter's skirt to keep her alive and away from the wave. We got out safely and went to Chennai, but it was a miraculous escape."

A picture of the tsunami hitting the Maldives

Pictures of damage done by the tsunami in Chennai, India

Back in Thailand, things were bad and getting worse. As Rick Von Feldt later reported to his family from the safety of his hotel high above the sea, "The water receded slight - and then, again with a vengeance. Rushed forward - rose again - and the 18 feet wall rolled over the front of the beach - the shops and everything in its path. We stood there in disbelief ... but realizing that one of the most awful things that could happen - just had. But it wasn't over ... It would recede - and then come again - rushing over the seawall. We could see that people in the hotels were climbing as quickly as they could. They huddled on the roofs of all the hotels. And down below - we could see boats and autos and everything smaller being thrashed again and again against buildings. It looked like a bathtub with lots of small toys - surreal - but real enough. Four hours ... battering the sea front. Yet the sun kept shining. A very deceptive paradise."

Of course, what Von Feldt observed from safety most people in the area experienced up close and personal. Mark Nelson, yet another tourist in Thailand for holiday, became aware of the tsunami when he saw a fish swimming in his hotel. "I was laying in bed in the Ban Thai resort on Patong Beach [and] my friend was showering as we heard this huge noise, a fight? I looked out of our upgraded first floor room to the pool /patio and saw nothing but water, filled with small fish and floating sundries. A broken pipe was my first thought; I pulled out bottles of shampoo trying to save the pool guy more work from the clean-up. It just got worse and worse ... we dashed up the back flight of stairs as wave 2 or 3 swept around our hotel ... I went into the water to pull out a man. 'Let me get you to your room,' I said. 'This is not my hotel,' he responded. 'Where did you come from?' 'I was just walking on the beach and now I'm here,' came his response ... His legs were mangled [so] I wrapped him in a bed sheet from a toppled maids cart and set him in the lobby. I never saw him again. When I returned a boat was sitting where the lobby bench had been."

Mark Brandon also had his first brush with the mighty wave while inside a hotel: "I was wondering what to do when I saw people screaming and running past the glass reception doors toward the main beach road (the main road is about 5 meters from the reception area). Someone opened the glass reception door and I stepped out. Immediately, I saw water everywhere. This was, as I understand it now, the first wave and the only warning of what was about to come. I looked to the left and saw behind what it was from which people were running. It was a massive wave of gray foam moving up in between the bungalows with devastating power and speed. In its wake was a lot of debris and I estimated the wave to be around 3 – 4 meters high. It wasn't so much the height of the wave, but its crushing power and speed that I remember more vividly; anyway, I didn't stop to look. I knew immediately what it was and turned to run in the opposite direction, diagonally across the road and up an alley, oblivious to any traffic, as fast as I could, losing my flip-flops along the way. The alley came to a dead end. There were a few trees around and a small wall, which I thought of climbing over; but the water, up to my thighs at this time, didn't seem to be getting any higher and had started to recede slightly, so I stayed where I was. I reckon I was about 50 meters inland from the hotel reception area. ...The water, from where I stood, was completely black in color. It was hard to believe that this was a tidal wave or tsunami; it was more like all the underground sewage systems had exploded."

Meanwhile, back in his office, Dave Lowe was trying to save himself and others, but part of the problem was processing information that seemed to make no sense, like thousands of gallons of water rushing past office equipment. Moreover, people in the office had little time to think: "I ran towards reception, where guests and staff were screaming and rooted to the spot as the first waves began to hit the island. The furniture was already being swept away, and the guest shop window exploded, showering glass into the water where guests without shoes were trying to stand up.... Within seconds the water was up to my waist, and as I braced myself for what seemed like certain death, the tsunami wave slammed into the resort, crushing me against the walls of the executive offices ... As I desperately inched my way to reception, with water roiling and boiling so violently I could hardly stand up. It was like a vortex, and I grabbed hold of children who were being washed out to sea and whose parents were missing, and threw them up onto the reception counter. As I looked back to see if I could help anyone else, the full force of the tsunami hit, crushing palm trees and instantly destroying the executive offices whose windows smashed. And then the walls collapsed, sending staff trapped inside...straight out to sea. I grabbed hold of a pillar as the wave struck, and the water was now up to my chest ... Most guests were clinging to anything they could find, and some had horrible injuries from the smashed glass that was everywhere."

Pictures of damage in Sri Lanka

Chapter 5: The Life Taking Swell

"The second - and most deadly swell came. And this one was the life taking swell. Larger. More fierce. Taller by 10 feet - this one just came so strongly - and pushed everything in its path towards the town. People were but leaves going under. This swell pushed all of the 200 cars on the beach forward. It pushed hundreds of parked motorcycles and tuk tuks. It pushed over the two busses parked in front of the dive ... It pushed hard and strong. Everything was pushed into the first row of hotels and shops lining the beach. The swirls first broke open window and doors and washing out every stick of furniture ... And then every hole of room space was replaced with larger items. Autos were thrown against buildings. Where there was a bed was now a car. Or 3 mangled motorcycles. The Coco-cola truck delivering morning soda was picked up and ran into the side of a bank, wedging it so tight into the lobby that four vehicles the next day would have to pull it out. Boats on the ocean were thrown into the forks of tall palm trees on the beach."
- Rick Von Feldt

Pictures of beached boats in Indonesia

As the water gushed inland in all directions, it swept along seemingly everything in its path, and within a matter of minutes, thousands of men, women and children living around the Indian Ocean went from living their lives to fighting to live. Von Feldt recalled, "People at the Starbucks went screaming madly. In 10 seconds, every piece of coffee equipment, chair, table and bags of coffee were washed away. The only thing remaining were the lights hanging from the second story ceiling. The water weaved its way for 4 blocks inland - getting caught like a guided stream between banks of buildings. The force pushed between the buildings, rising as high as 10 feet down perpendicular roads to the beach - again, washing out everything shop on the ground floor. And the people? Few had a real chance. If you could swim - and managed to follow the wave - you might have a chance. But even if you could swim, the items being thrown with you - above you - under you - battered you. Glass from many of the store front windows flowed silently and cut people. If you were lucky enough to get away from the first wave - and you ran upstairs to tops of buildings, you might have been lucky. But on Phuket beach - nearly 500 people who were on the beach never made it. Families. Seniors. Fisherman. 250 bodies have been found so far. More just disappeared."

The problem was that most of those who survived the first large wave were killed or at least swept away just a few minutes later by the second deadly wave. Von Feldt continued, "Because once all that water flowed inland during the second SWELL - the ocean once again, pulled back, and drained the city just as fast - pulling out once again. People talk of two waves. The incoming was tough. But once the water from the second wave pulled back, everything floating in that water had to fall. Half of it flowed back out to sea, like a hand of a monster grabbing - and not letting go. The rest fell to the ground as the water vacated. Debris stacked 3 feet high covered everything. And the rest just washed out to sea - only to be returned, each morning, little by little. And the whole while, the morning sunshine warmed the day."

For many, especially those who were visiting the area from other parts of the world, it seemed that nothing this grave could actually be taking place. People often apply their accumulated life experiences to new situations to try to judge what is actually happening, and Mark Oberle was one of them. He described what it was like: "I heard an explosion and saw a roiling black mass of water next to a waterfront hotel. I thought it was a sewer line breaking. Mardie thought it was a dam failure, and many others thought it was a terrorist attack. Quickly after there were more distant explosions to the north up the beach, sounding like canon fire. The 'explosions' were from the initial large wave slapping into the concrete buildings as the wave successively reached different points up the beach. Then I saw a swell of floodwater heading our way--- perhaps just a 3-4 foot deep plateau of water with a roiling mass of water and debris at the leading edge. Then I finally realized it was a tsunami, related to the earthquakes two hours earlier. However, even at that point I thought it was a small tsunami and did not understand the magnitude of the disaster because our view of the coast was blocked by the intervening palms and line of beachfront hotels. We went up to our second floor room and saw the floodwaters quickly fill up the courtyard around the pool, carrying chairs, palm fronds and other debris with it. A few minutes later a second, higher wave of floodwater entered the courtyard and filled the pool with mud and debris. The water eventually reached the lower edge of the sliding glass door to the room below us. ... A sinkhole started to form underneath the patio below our room, and floodwater rushed under the building."

Whether he realized it at that moment or not, Oberle was one of the lucky ones, since he was able to observe what was happening from at least some safety. Dave Lowe was close to the shore, and he also happened to be the lone person in charge of an increasingly dangerous situation. He wrote, "Then, as quickly as the water came up, it was gone, leaving fish flopping on the floor of the lobby and seaweed draped everywhere. I shouted at staff to get a guest list for a head count, and screamed at guests ... As guests regrouped, I looked out to sea in the opposite direction, where my eyes popped out of their head: there was another wave coming right back at us, even bigger than the first, and even worse, full of air conditioners, refrigerators, water heaters, mattresses deck chairs, and even people ... I screamed as guests ran for things to grab hold of. When the 2nd wave hit, it was like titanic, and we desperately tried to hang on as the dangerous debris smashed its way through the lobby again. This was followed by two more waves, which were slightly smaller, and then silence. As I assembled guests together for a head count, a staff from the other end of the island ran in and said that there was a 50 foot wave coming, and we needed to get to the spa, where there was more shelter."

Once someone was in the water, it was nearly impossible to get out. Felix later remembered how just being able to swim was not enough because there was so much debris to fight through: "I saw my friends Louise and Zac in front of me jumping onto a high step and into a shop and as I jumped up to follow them I saw another wave rushing towards us from the other side of the island. The next second we were all under water being tossed around, as if we were in a huge washing machine full of rubble. I could see furniture and bodies but no light and couldn't figure out which way was up."

Many others quickly found themselves caught in the surging tides, and their challenge was to find something solid to cling to before being washed away. Fiona described her fight for survival and nearly miraculous triumph: "Then the wave hit me. I still wasn't particularly scared at this point as all I was thinking was 'It's just water, and I can swim – I will be fine.' Immediately I got caught in its force and found myself tumbling along the ground completely out of control. It was at that point that I realized that I could die. The next thing I remember is looking up at the sky through the water and seeing some tangled mangrove roots and thinking that I had to try to hoist myself up through the trees in order to breathe. That was where I stayed. I think I might have lost consciousness for a bit at that point, because it seemed that almost immediately to me everything then went eerily quiet and I was the only person on the whole island. I tried to pull myself up from the mangrove trees, and realized quickly that I was completely trapped and couldn't go anywhere."

Chapter 6: Bloodied and Battered People

Pictures of flooding and damage in Malaysia

"From up the hill came bloodied and battered people. As the waves would retreat for 10-15 minutes, many people would try to make a run for it - and run down the beach side street the edge - where climbed sharply - and where we were standing. ... For two hours - the waves ebbed and flowed - crossing over the edge - pushing and pulling items. But none were as strong as the first two tidal waves - that so destructively threw cars on top of each other - overturned busses - and washed out every stick of furniture.... As people left the beach, and walked up the hill in shock, our hotel became a sort of refugee camp. The road filled with wet people – in shock - bloody - with broken arms and legs. People cried and cried. Others sat at the edge of the road (between our hotel and the cliff that overlooked the beach). But instead of watching what was happening below - they turned away - not wanting to relive over and over what they had been through. Everyone was confused. We had heard nothing. The weather was beautiful. What on earth could be happening?" - Rick Von Feldt

Of all the people that lived through that dreadful day, few came as close to dying as Sally Huyton. She explained, "I thought that if I could get to the concrete stair case next to the gym, I would be OK ... I got pushed sideways into the gym which was glass fronted and faced the sea ... The next thing I remember was looking up behind me and all the glass surrounding me exploded. … Within a second, the whole gym was filled to the ceiling with black water. … It was like being in a washing machine with all sorts of gym equipment, wooden sun loungers, trees, glass, boats, everything. I could feel myself getting banged from every angle but I couldn't feel any pain. I was more bothered about holding my breath. I don't know how long I was under the water but it felt like a lifetime. I was exhausted. I couldn't hold my breath any longer. I started to think about Paul and my mum and dad and how upset they would be if I died, but I couldn't hold on anymore … I then thought this is it, I'm going to die, my time is up. I relaxed, went limp and started to breathe in the water. It was very easy to do (didn't taste nice though). It may sound corny but it was really peaceful, like in a euphoric state. I remember seeing a bright light underneath me and brief flashes of my life, cheesy I know but true."

More than 150,000 died that day, in places ranging from the elegant beaches of Thailand to the fishing villages of India and even in violent towns along the coast of Somalia. Given that it was impossible to account for everyone missing, it's been estimated that as many as 280,000 or more actually died. However, Huyton was fortunate to not be one of them. She explained, "The next thing I remember is waking up in a basement full of rubbish and bodies. I wasn't on the floor because I could see water and bodies under me. I was coughing up lots of water and sick. I couldn't breathe very well, very short sharp breaths and I had gym equipment and weight benches on top of my legs … I tried to shout for help but I didn't have the energy. I could feel that there was something big sticking about 1 foot out of my side…. Then I looked up to my left and saw a doorway with half a staircase, I had to get up there if I wanted to get out. Then I heard water and looked up, more water rushed passed the door and the water underneath me started to rise … I pulled the piece of glass out of my stomach, and just went crazy wriggling my legs until eventually I got free. I scrambled over all the rubble and managed to pull myself up onto the staircase and walked out of the door. It was so bright and sunny but deadly silent. I was in a big hall, stood on a stage, all 3 double doors had been blasted off and all the chairs and tables were stacked up on one side of the room."

Sally wasn't the only one threatened by the next big wave. Dave Lowe, having called out to his guests to take cover, saw another frightening sight and dashed forward to try to prevent more death. "I heard a seaplane land, probably unaware of the danger. I ran like hell to the jetty, waving my arms to the pilots to tell them to go away…. They did not see me, and landed…. As they tied up to the pontoon, I noticed an ominous wave heading straight for the plane, and like a horror movie, I actually saw the seaplane getting sucked under by the vortexes and eddies that were 20 feet across … I screamed at the cabin crew who was on the dock, frantically trying to untie the rope, as the engines screaming, got closer and closer to the water. I got down on my hands and knees, covering my head with my hand to prevent injury, screaming into the walkie talkie to see if anyone could contact the pilots … I was just waiting for the engines to smash into the water and see the plane flip over, when the crew cut the rope, jumped on board, and the plane bobbed up and took off. As I watched it take off, they dipped their wings to show us help was on the way … I looked behind me to see a 5th wave bearing straight down, and as I ran back to reception, I was too late, and I was lifted off my feet and carried by it straight into the lobby again."

As the last of the biggest waves swooped back out to sea, those who had survived the crisis thus far began to turn their attention to rescuing others. Lowe felt heavily the burden of responsibility for both his employees and the guests at the resort. "When the wave subsided, I ran to the spa, passing the GM's house, where his son's nanny was nearly being washed away, I rescued her and his son, carried them to safety, where 60 terrified French, Italian and UK guests were huddled in total shock. Quickly I set up a triage unit to treat the broken bones and horrible cuts. Half the guests there were missing family, and were threatening me with death if I didn't let them get to see where they were, but the island had been cut in half, a river of water was now bisecting it, both ends of the island had lost 50 meters of land and coconut trees were being washed out to sea. For the next 6 hours, we rode out wave after wave as the sea gradually calmed down, but at least 5 warnings came to us via radio that a huge wave was still coming, 100 feet, 200 feet high."

The strongest of the survivors began to mobilize help for the weakest and the most seriously injured. The first job, of course, was to find the people who needed help and get them to somewhere where they could receive care. Luke Simmonds was very fortunate to be one of the strongest ones, and he remembered, "At the Cabana Hotel we started to make a hospital area. Some people came on their own, others we heard screaming and we went to them. Another English guy called CC was a psychiatrist, and so we kind of appointed him in charge. The first girl we collected from the rubble was an English girl called Sally. She was covered in the most severe cuts I have ever seen. Imagine those documentaries about liposuction, etc. ... Gaping holes with grotesque cuts in the flesh, to the bone. She had at least 7 lacerations over her legs and tummy."

The young woman, Sally, that Simmons mentioned was none other than Sally Huyton. Still in the destroyed gym, she recalled, "I stood there for a second then looked down, I was stood in a big pool of blood which I imagined was mine so I thought I'd best lie down. As I lay there I gathered all my energy and managed to shout for help. ... Then I saw a man stood in the doorway with a lifejacket on, it was Luke Simmonds. ... He put me on a door and a few of them carried me to safety. He asked me how I was and at that stage I thought I had punctured a lung and broken my ankle. Little did I know that I had a hole in my stomach that you could fit 2 big fists in, my foot was hanging off and from my waist down to the back of my knee looked like a shark had eaten it. I had holes a few inches long all over my body and had lost a lot of blood. ... Luke covered me with sheets to keep the flies off and I remember him pouring alcohol into my stomach which hurt like hell! Luke held my hand and looked after me until Paul found me, which was a couple of hours later."

Due to the adrenaline and shock, many people were walking around the island despite being terribly wounded, and though her injuries kept her from walking, even Sally had no idea just how hurt she was. She explained, "To see Paul's face was unbelievable, I felt like I had a smile from ear to ear but I was told that I didn't and that I was fighting for breath. I felt happy inside, not thinking for one minute that I may still die so Luke made sure that I was on the first boat off the island."

Chapter 7: Taken to a Hospital

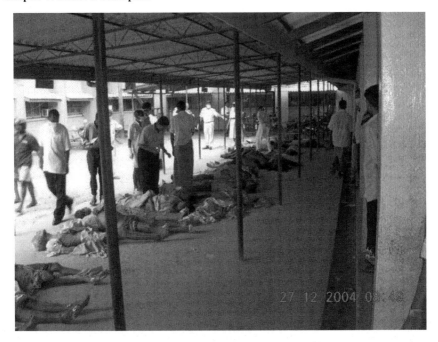

"I was the first person to be taken off the boat but the medics kept grabbing my foot and the pain go so bad I went to pass out. Then a little old Thai lady ran out of the crowd and put smelling salts under my nose until I came too. I was taken to a hospital in Phuket and operated on. I thought the nightmare was over but I came to whilst they were still operating on my ankle, the pain was unbearable, but they had to continue. The next day Ralph showed up…. The woman who came with Ralph arranged for an ambulance to drive from Bangkok for 12 hours to pick me up and drive me back to Bumrungrad hospital. That same night a couple from Jersey where we live, also good friends of my aunty and uncle, turned up at the hospital. They had been staying in Phuket at the time. That was also amazing to see friendly faces. Whilst in recovering in Bangkok, I then got pneumonia so I spent about 3-4 weeks there before I could fly home." - Sally Huyton

As the immediate threat of flooding subsided and those who had been injured began to move about or be rescued, the next step was to provide some sort of first aid to keep them alive until more help could arrive. With no real way available at the moment to get to medical facilities, many individuals began to set up makeshift first aid stations around the area, using whatever was on hand to help the injured. Fiona soon realized she was among those who most needed help: "Simon managed to pull me out of the mangrove trees so that I was lying on top of them. That was when we realized that my leg was in a much worse state then we had originally thought. The tibia was snapped completely, like a twig, and all the skin on my lower leg seemed to have sloughed away. I could also see red stinging ants climbing around in my muscle and whatever else was left of my leg, and my thigh was starting to swell up. I couldn't feel any pain at all at first, and that was strange, but after a few minutes the pain started up and got worse and worse. … There was a little concrete hut a few feet into the forest, and they decided to carry me there ... The bottom of my leg was hanging onto the rest of it by a small piece of skin at the back, and every time they tried to carry me it would flop down and I would scream with pain. … We got to the hut, and it was completely packed with very badly injured people."

The chaos in the makeshift shelter was even worse than what remained outside. No one on the island was completely well, as even those who were uninjured were in a state of shock over what they had seen or worried sick over missing loved ones. Thus, instead of finding the help she had hoped for, Fiona found herself in a new sort of hell with desperate people, many of whom were more severely injured than she was. She continued, "The only place to lie me down was in the doorway. … I remember there was a woman there who was lying on a makeshift bed. Her husband was kneeling over her side and was shouting at everyone asking them if they know how to do mouth to mouth. Simon went over to try to help, but she was dead. I was losing a lot of blood and was gradually starting to feel more and more out of it. At some point, our tour guide came to the hut, and…taking one look at me…came back with a yellow canoe ... They lifted me into the canoe and started carrying me towards the beach again. … We later found out that I was the only survivor from that hut. 20 people died on the island that day. The man who had found the canoe slid me over the beach and then jumped into the canoe, paddling it himself. There was no room for Si in the canoe and so he held onto the back of it and started swimming. … Every time the Thai man who was paddling me looked at my leg he threw up into the sea. All three of us were petrified there was going to be another wave. We eventually got to the speed boat, and it went back to the mainland as quickly as possible."

Even those who were uninjured were in desperate circumstances, as most of the buildings on the shores had been damaged or destroyed. Again, this situation was especially critical for those who were in Thailand on vacation, as they did not have friends or family they could turn to at the time. While it is true that most people who died that dreadful day drowned, many others were fatally injured by cuts, internal injuries and head trauma from being hit by the debris the water was shooting into all parts of the coast. Luke Simmonds worked to create a triage area to deal with those awaiting proper help, and he remembered, "They just kept coming. A Japanese husband and wife. The wife had lost half of her throat. We simply held her neck together. A Swedish women whose head was cleaved open - we tied her head together. A Japanese girl whose leg was so badly broken, we decided that we had to put it straight. I held her hand, and kissed her, whilst crying with her, as 3 guys pulled her leg straight. It took 3 or 4 minutes of the most unbelievable pain for this girl. She was amazing … Afterwards we all prayed for the rest of her group. She was missing 16 people! Then there was an Israeli boy, travelling on his own, I think called Tommy. He had a major cut by his armpit and was petrified that he would lose his arm. I cleaned out his wound whilst trying to give reassurance. I'm pretty sure he would be OK as he was able to move everything … It just looked so horrible. Whilst we were helping someone, often you would hear, 'Doctor, please come and help my friend.' I didn't know whether to explain that I wasn't a Doctor or not. 9 times out of 10, I said I wasn't, but still people were desperate for help."

As much as Simmonds and others tried to help the injured, the only hope for most people was to get to a hospital. Fiona was lucky in a way, since she was one of the first to make it back to the mainland of Thailand. She later recalled, "When we got back there I was almost unconscious. Luckily as we were so early there was an ambulance waiting and it took me straight to Krabi hospital. I lost Si when we got to the shore, but apparently the minute he saw me being taken into the ambulance, he collapsed. His leg was much more badly injured than he had originally thought, and he spent the next month in hospital himself. I have very little memory of the next 2 days apart from being hot, being in pain, hearing people screaming and moaning, asking for water and painkillers, and being too scared to look at my leg."

Chapter 8: Back to Reality

"It was total chaos, but after a few hours we got on a bus to the airport and after another few hours we were flown by military jet to Bangkok. It looked like the sort of plane that might fly tanks and for one horrible minute I thought they might make us parachute out at the other end! British Embassy staff were waiting at Bangkok airport and we finally got the chance to phone home to say we were ok. Then it was on to the Landmark Hotel courtesy of the Thai government where we stayed for two days while we sorted out new passports and some clothes. We decided then to carry on with our trip, not go home and sit watching terrible news footage (and I didn't want my son's lasting memory of Thailand to be the Tsunami) and we actually managed to have a very lovely two weeks in Koh Samui! Then it was back to reality and the realisation that, but for the grace of God, we could have just had our last ever holiday." - Felix in Phi Phi

Pictures of rubble in Indonesia

Even those who were not injured knew they needed to get away from all the death and destruction as soon as possible. This was especially true of parents travelling with their children, as they were concerned about the permanent scars the young ones might have from exposure to such horror.

Among the last to leave the island were those in charge of the care of others. Dave Lowe quickly began to try to put together some sort of makeshift shelter for the people he was responsible for. He explained, "Guests suffered in the strong sun, and we found a tarp to create a shelter for the 15 children without parents. That evening, when we had got all guests together, we sandbagged the restaurant and set up all night patrols to watch the sea. No one slept that night. We were terrified of a wave hitting in darkness, and all night we just huddled in corners waiting for sunrise. Someone produced a flashlight, and with the guests secure, we checked out our rooms, which has been totally demolished, everything washed out to sea. When the sun came up, there were champagne bottles, passports, candy bars, dinner plates, business cards and hundreds of branches and tree trunks washed up on the beach. Within 4 hours we had evacuated the guests on two huge speedboats and as soon as the last guest left, the staff took off our nametags, and just burst into tears. We didn't get off the island until 2 days later, and we salvaged what we could of our belongings, some things washed up on the beach, some things wrapped around trees, and some things covered in mud. We showered in the sea and rationed the bottled water we had left. When we boarded the seaplanes to get back to Male, and we flew over the destroyed island, the full devastation was clear. Over 100 rooms demolished, no restaurants intact, and debris and trash was everywhere. It wasn't until that evening that we heard the death toll and the devastation elsewhere."

Pictures of rubble in Thailand

Of course, most of the people could not leave the devastated areas because they were natives. Instead, they had to do the best they could to rebuild and take back what they had lost. During the months and even years that followed, millions of dollars would pour in from all over the world to help people rebuild, but no amount of money could bring back the dead, or restore the lost beaches. In the wake of the tsunami, one native of Jakarta, Indonesia observed, "One famous reporter from the biggest news TV station here cried her heart out when reporting live from Banda Aceh, she was devastated. The city's like a huge dumpster, dead bodies still scattered everywhere, debris blocking the streets with possibly victims of the tsunami in those piles. Help hasn't arrived yet even there in the capital of Aceh. People who are hungry tried to break in one grocery store only to find food covered in mud and water and bodies of people who couldn't escape at the time the tsunami hit."

Likewise, a resident in the Maldives drew attention to the plight of many when he noted, "We are badly affected. Numbers of low-lying islands are almost submerged. The local people are seeking refuge in small dhonis. Most of the islands are out of electricity, food and water and the sewage system is totally destroyed. The government is totally unable to send help to these small islands. Many islanders have to spend the night outside since so many houses have been destroyed."

Still, there is no situation so bad that some good does not come out of it. Months after the tsunami hit, the Oxford Mail carried the following story: "An Oxford university student is leaving behind ambitions of becoming a City banker to marry a Thai man who helped her cling to life after the Asian tsunami. Naomi Bowman, 21, was swept off the beach on the island of Koh Phi Phi, sustaining a large gash to her body, two broken ribs and extensive cuts to her head and thighs. She was operated on six times under general anesthetic after the Boxing Day tragedy which claimed around 300,000 lives in countries around the Indian Ocean. She still struggles to walk. But her harrowing experiences in Thailand have not dissuaded her from returning - for love is pulling her back. Now Naomi, a maths undergraduate, has decided to scrap her high-flying career dreams and spend the rest of her life with 30-year-old Theep Janthamanee, a rock climbing teacher whom she had befriended before the disaster. After searching for Naomi for three days, Theep found her in a crowded hospital, she told the Mail on Sunday. 'Because of a lack of medical staff, he fed me, dressed my wounds, helped me to walk and move again and even changed my bed pans,' she said. 'At night when I could not sleep he lay by my side and comforted me. Now I want to spend the rest of my life with Theep. If it were not for him, I might not be here. He is so caring and compassionate, so wonderful and careful; I just fell in love with him.'"

If only all the other victims could have been so lucky.

Bibliography

Krauss, Erich. (2005) *Wave of Destruction: The Stories of Four Families and History's Deadliest Tsunami.* Rodale Books.

Lace, William. (2008) *The Indian Ocean Tsunami of 2004.* Chelsea House.

Lee, Tracey and Lucy Popescu. (2013) *Tsunami 2004.* Nickerson Publishing.

Owens, Patricia. (2014) *Tsunami Journal 2004.* Amazon Digital Services.

Printed in Great Britain
by Amazon